# FROM ARROWHEADS TO IRRIGATORS

## A History of Frilford and Collins Farm

## Murray Maclean

MURRAY MACLEAN
COLLINS FARM   FRILFORD
NR ABINGDON   OXON

*British Library Cataloguing-in-Publication Data.*
*A catalogue record for this book is available*
*from the British Library.*

ISBN 978-1-5262-0575-9
*Printed in Great Britain by*
*Arthur H. Stockwell Ltd*
*Torrs Park    Ilfracombe*
*Devon  EX34 8BA*

# INTRODUCTION

Some while after joining my father as a fruit grower, in late 1959, a girlfriend gave me a cutting of a poem taken from a farming magazine. The words made such an impression upon me that I framed the poem; it still hangs on the office wall.

It has taken many more years of working on the land for the full impact of those powerful words to embed themselves deep into my subconscious. The second verse is the most relevant to the above title:

> Now I am come at last to my own land
> And my own people – I have found my place
> Among the weather-wary, wise-eyed men
> That, in these quiet fields have planted, dark,
> Long years of laughter and mute agony –
> Regret and rye grass, barley and young love.
>
> Now, in the new-stained hollow of my hand
> I hold fast my inheritance – this soil
> Grown sharply sweet with the smell of centuries.
> My ancient fathers knew it – it was mine
> Before I was, because of them . . . and what they lost
> In leaving, it lay dormant in their seed
> To grow in me a solitude and hunger of the heart.
>
> The drifting wood-smoke ghosts the leaning field –
> Its bitter fragrance quenching my long thirst,
> Balm for my hurt, a seal for my content.
> And I am lost no more – I am come home.

*Helen Morgan*

3

I had been involved with the growing of fruit crops on part of the land at Collins Farm, Frilford, since 1959; but I did not become the owner of the complete small farm until 1969.

Over the past forty-plus years I have accumulated a collection of old objects found in the soil as we worked, bending down, to plant, weed and harvest the crops – coins, pottery shards, flints, buttons, bullets, clay pipes, sheep bells, pieces of glass, numerous horseshoes and small pieces of old farm machinery. The most beautiful being a perfect flint arrowhead that dates back to the late Neolithic age (approximately 2500 BC).

These fragments from past generations provide a unique link to those unknown people who cultivated the land before me and have spawned a desire to research the part that they played in the evolution of the landscape of this farm and its immediate surroundings.

It has been a journey of discovery through the past centuries, but there remain large gaps in available information on the history of Frilford from the Middle Ages right up to the early Victorian era of land Enclosure Acts; however, I will show that the very late enclosure of the parish, in 1861, gave the local farmers the freedom and impetus to invest in their newly amalgamated holdings to improve both the cropping and the profitability of their endeavours. My searches will show how the landscape has evolved and the changing uses to which the land has been subject since that flint arrowhead fell to the ground over 4,000 years ago.

# 1

# WHO SHAPED THE LANDSCAPE OF FRILFORD?

## Topography

The parish of Frilford is uniformly level and gently undulating land as part of the open landscape of the upper Corallian limestone ridge. This ridge runs, east to west, along the northern side of the Vale of the White Horse, before sloping steeply down into the Thames Valley.

A light sandy loam overlies the coral rag limestone, which comes close to the surface in some areas making deep cultivations difficult. However, these characteristics provide a free-draining, light, easy-working soil that would have been well suited to the limited capabilities of the early cultivators of this landscape.

The River Ock runs along the southern boundary of the parish, whilst the smaller Piling Brook runs across the northern side, providing water for the hamlet and running on into the neighbouring parish of Marcham, where it joins the River Ock.

## Land Clearance and Use

Archaeological evidence indicates that man first arrived in the locality during the Neolithic era as a hunter, whose flint tools and weapons have been found on the dry gravel terraces alongside the River Thames. Excavations at Yarnton, near Oxford, have provided a lot of information about early settlement in the area from which later generations would have moved 'inland' to begin clearing the mixed-woodland cover, to be able to graze their cattle on the dry higher land. A beautiful late-Neolithic (approximately 2500 BC) flint arrowhead found on Collins Farm is indicative of that movement away from the river terraces. In the fields to the west of the farm lie the outlines of Iron Age hut circles and enclosure ditches which have been identified by aerial photography. (*See the site marked on Map A, north of the Roman villa site.*)

*A fine Neolithic flint arrowhead found on Collins Farm, 2.5 cm long.*

In 1884 the archaeologist Arthur Evans excavated a Roman villa site lying in open farmland a quarter of a mile due south of the Iron Age huts site. The villa comprised thirteen rooms, one of which had hypocaust under-floor heating. Some way from the villa stood a small bathhouse, draining into a little pond. Aerial surveys of this part of the parish indicate numerous crop marks showing that large areas had been extensively cleared and cropped during the Roman occupation.

It is a realistic assumption that when the Romans first arrived into the area they would have chosen to set up their farm and villa on land that had already been cleared and was easy to cultivate. The light and free-draining land is ideal for grazing livestock outdoors throughout the winter months without causing any lasting damage to the soil structure. During the dry summer months these same animals would have been moved down onto nearby pastureland beside the small Piling Brook to the north or the larger River Ock to the south. Both these watercourses are within easy reach of the central plateau, making the present parish an ideal site for early settlement. (*See Map A.*)

The excellent topographical features for settlement sites within the parish are further proven by the presence of a substantial Roman temple half a mile to the south of the present hamlet. The temple site also contains a large circular, amphitheatre-like, structure and other buildings, which add significantly to the importance of the whole area. It has been discovered that this whole complex was built on top of an earlier Iron Age settlement.

The extensive settlement of the area since the middle of the Iron Age indicates that the surrounding countryside would have been largely cleared of its original mixed oak, birch and thorn woodland (with hazel and alder on lower-lying land) to allow for simple cultivations, grazing of livestock and to provide fuel for domestic fires.

The Roman temple complex contains evidence of furnaces for small metalworking, probably for the manufacture of trinkets to be sold as offerings to the gods. The wood required for the furnaces for the manufacture of pottery and the presence of metalworking would have also contributed to land clearance in the wider landscape.

The evidence from recent aerial surveys shows that both the Iron Age and later Roman farmers used small enclosures with attendant trackways for the management of their livestock. Larger, uniform-shaped enclosures could have been big enough for crop production.

Ritual burials of both cattle and sheep found within the Frilford temple complex indicate the importance of livestock to the local community. The skeleton of a cow was much smaller than most present-day commercial breeds; its size being more akin to a Dexter, thus giving us an insight to the possible type of breeds of the period.

Evidence from archaeological sites throughout Britain indicates that the transition of the lowland landscape of southern

England from its 'original' woodland/forest state would have been a gradual clearance of the land as man evolved from a roaming hunter-gatherer to becoming settled in communities based upon the management of livestock. Cattle, sheep and pigs provided both food and clothing. The cultivation of crops was a further evolution of land use and resulted from the combination of settlement and woodland clearance.

## Community Boundaries

We do not know precisely how or when our present-day system of community boundaries evolved, but the present layout of parish boundaries did develop in the post-Roman revival of rural England under a succession of Anglo-Saxon kings. As in previous centuries, the changes resulted from the continuing evolution of land use based upon the specific needs of the period. Expanding local communities would have needed to formalise, and secure, agreed boundaries within which they could husband their livestock, grow their crops and obtain vital supplies of water, timber and forage for the livestock.

The map of the parish of Frilford with its adjacent neighbours (Map A) shows how care and consideration had been taken in its layout.

The parish of Kingston Bagpuize, to the west, is an excellent example of the perfect layout. The long, thin parish borders the River Thames in the north and stretches southward to the River Ock, with the community living on the dry high ground in the middle of the parish. The villagers could drive their livestock equal distances, be it to north or south, to reach water and summer grazing meadows. In the winter stock could be out-wintered on grass or crop stubbles close to the village. Woodland is still to be found between the village and the respective water sources. The community was thus self-sufficient for its primary food and fuel resources.

The parishes of Frilford and Marcham, its larger neighbour to the east, both share the River Ock to the south as their major

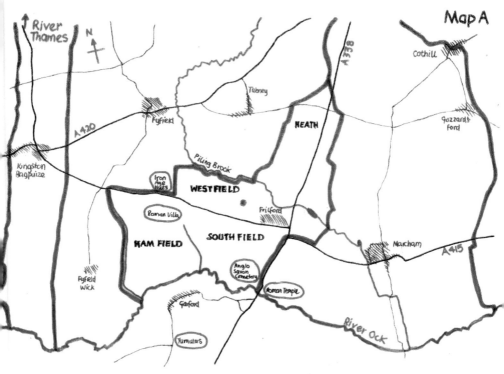

*MAP A – Parish boundaries are outlined in green.*
*The River Ock (bottom, running west to east) and Piling Brook (top, running south and eastwards) are outlined in blue. Archaeological sites are ringed in red or shown as a red dot. Note the Iron Age settlement site, just outside the Frilford parish boundary, to the north of the Roman villa site in the centre of Ham Field. The Roman temple complex is just outside the eastern parish boundary, with its adjacent Romano-British cemetery just inside the parish. The red dot in West Field is a 'non- existent' burial mound, which has only recently appeared on DEFRA maps of Collins Farm, and probably relates to the work of the archaeologist Richard Hingley, who lived in Frilford in his youth. It was he who was largely instrumental in revealing the 'amphitheatre', near to the Roman temple, and thus the importance of this large religious site. A tumulus is identified in Garford parish, together with the recently discovered site of another Roman villa to the south-east, on the other side of the known Roman road running north from Wantage towards Oxford (A338).*

9

water source together with the adjacent area of low-lying summer pasture. To the north the smaller Piling Brook feeds directly through the centre of both communities, providing water for household needs. In the northern part of both parishes lies a large expanse of acid heath and woodland from which timber for building needs, and forage in the form of gorse and bracken, could be cut to provide supplementary livestock winter feed and bedding. Thus the original layout of these local parish boundaries took account of the requirements of the respective communities for their basic needs to sustain themselves and their livestock. (*See Map A.*)

## Place Names in a Farming Landscape

The name for the hamlet of Frilford is likely to have derived from its association with the Ock river crossing or 'ford'. The first part of the name – 'Fril' – was recorded in the Domesday Book as 'Frieliford', which could refer to an Anglo-Saxon name, 'Frithila', indicating a continuity of identity with its Bronze Age and Roman past.

Some parish field names appear in an agreement dated 6 June 1735, where references are made to Tuckpen, Millingditch and Emead. The location of only one has been established to date.

**Tuckpen** – this could refer to an enclosure belonging to a person called Tuck. It does not provide any clue to a possible connection with a landscape feature that would help to locate it today.

**Millingditch** – the River Ock is the only watercourse in the parish that would have been capable of providing an adequate water flow throughout the year to supply a working mill.

**Emead** – the old English word for a river or a large brook is '*ea*'. Fortunately in this instance we do know where the meadow was situated. Access to a very detailed Enclosure Award map for the parish drawn up in 1846 by W. H. Davies, surveyor from Abingdon, shows the Emead Furlong situated beside the Piling Brook along part of the northern boundary of West Field. This is confirmed by the document stating that these three meads were annexed to the South and West Fields of Frilford.

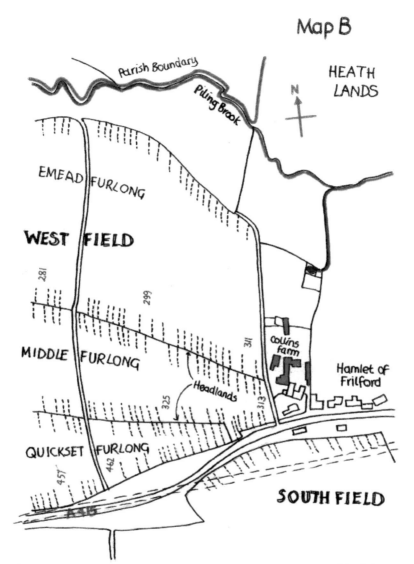

Map B

MAP B – A tracing from part of the Enclosure Award map of Frilford drawn up in 1846. The map shows the common fields, furlongs and strips (all of which are individually numbered on the original map). The section shown is part of the present Collins Farm, mentioned in the text. Note the two headland furlongs radiating westwards out from the hamlet and one directly out of Collins farmyard. The lower of the two, between Quickset and Middle Furlongs is still very visible as it crosses the farm heading westwards. The ends of the strips are shown; all measurements are recorded in chains (twenty-two yards). Most of the strips indicated are either one or two chains wide.

**South and West Fields** – these two large open fields referred to in the Enclosure Act are logically placed in the southern and western parts of the parish.

The other large field recorded on the enclosure map was called **Ham Field** – the old English word '*hamm*' refers to land hemmed in by marsh or water. This field is bordered on its west side by a small stream and on its east side is a marshy area of springs, both of which run south to join the River Ock. The only easy access to this field being from the road (today's A415) that runs along the higher, northern, side. The Roman villa was situated in the centre of this large field.


## Land Cultivation

During both the Celtic and Roman eras there had been a predominance of small, square enclosed fields that reflected the use of primitive ploughs, which were only capable of making a shallow furrow. Thus it is likely that they had to employ a system of multiple cultivations, ploughing and harrowing the ground in opposite directions until an adequate tilth was obtained. The geophysical surveys on Ham Field, the Roman villa site, clearly show uniform, larger, square enclosures suitable for cultivation. These enclosures could have been formed to exclude 'free-ranging' livestock from damaging their crops of wheat or barley.

The last Roman legions were withdrawn in AD 410, to deal with growing unrest closer to home, leaving the local inhabitants in the hands of the ruling Romano-British classes. To the west of, and opposite, the Roman temple site in Frilford is situated a Romano-British cemetery, which was first excavated in 1864/5. A further, more detailed, excavation was undertaken by D. Buxton in 1921. From the artefacts discovered, which included a number of lead coffins, this cemetery was in use from the late Roman period until the end of the sixth century. It demonstrates that an active community continued to live in this area into the early Anglo-Saxon period. (*See Map A.*)

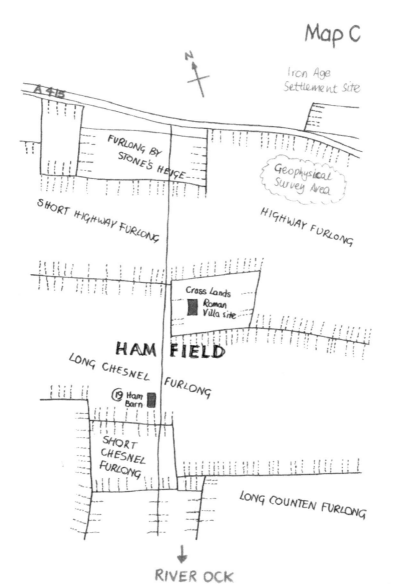

Map C

N

A 415

Iron Age
Settlement Site

FURLONG BY
STONE'S HENGE

Geophysical
Survey Area

SHORT HIGHWAY FURLONG

HIGHWAY FURLONG

Cross Lands
Roman
Villa site

HAM FIELD

LONG CHESNEL FURLONG

19 Ham
Barn

SHORT
CHESNEL
FURLONG

LONG COUNTEN FURLONG

RIVER OCK

*MAP C – A further tracing of another section of the 1846 Enclosure Award map;
this one shows the northern part of Ham Field. It highlights the interesting feature of
an isolated small block of strips surrounding the Roman villa site. Could these strips
have been laid out at a later date following the clearance of stone rubble remaining
from the villa's ruins? At the top of the map note the position of the Iron Age
settlement site to the north of the present road. To the south of the road is the area
subject to a recent geophysical survey, which was primarily carried out to verify
enclosures outlines identified by aerial surveys. The images on page 16 show that
the survey also brought to light the ploughing outlines of medieval strip cultivation.*

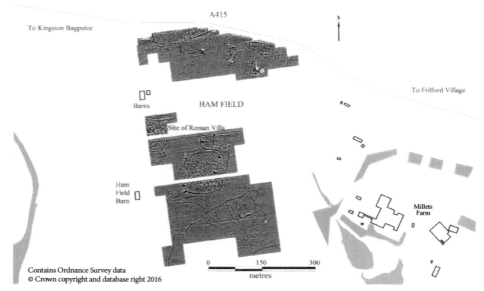

*An aerial survey of Ham Field revealed numerous outlines of former
enclosures dating back to the Roman era. These areas were subjected to
further geophysical surveys by William Wintle, who kindly supplied this copy
showing the extensive enclosures marks adjacent to the Roman villa site.*

Following the departure of the Romans there was a period of unrest
across the country as marauding bands of Saxons and Vikings raided
coastal communities and began to move inland. The eighth-century
monk and chronicler Bede recounts a time of severe upheaval
following the previous ordered society that had evolved during
nearly four centuries of influence and guidance from Rome.

As these marauding bands moved inland they began, in time,
to settle and create new 'immigrant' communities, integrating
with the resident populace to form the beginnings of what we now
term the Anglo-Saxon age. Lost skills would have been revived
alongside the new ideas and customs brought from northern
Germany by the Saxons.

Among the changes brought about by the arrival of the Saxons
was the way they cultivated the land. The Saxon farmer preferred
to utilise the strip cultivation methods they had used in Saxony.
These individual areas of cultivation were long and narrow strips
approximately 200 yards long and ten to fifteen yards wide;

the length and width varied according to local conditions and community preferences. Where possible they selected areas of level, free-draining and easy-working soils situated close to their simple dwellings. The limitations of the slow, lumbering oxen would have made it much harder work to cultivate sloping ground or the heavier, more-productive soils that are now favoured for the production of high-yielding cereal crops. The later introduction of iron shares and coulters to the wooden-framed ploughs improved the depth of ploughing and heralded the distinctive appearance of 'ridge-and-furrow' ploughing. Many signs of later medieval ridge-and-furrow strips remain to this day on heavy land sites that have escaped the plough in recent decades. The visible signs of the strips of ridged land with furrows between them arose from the practice of repeating the method of ploughing the same strip year after year on the same spot for generations.

We know that any visible evidence of the early strip cultivations in the Frilford parish have long since been erased by later ploughing methods. The detailed nineteenth-century enclosure map for the parish shows the fully developed three-field system of furlong strip cultivation. The word 'furlong' does not refer to its modern meaning of a length, but to an area. In the age of strip cultivation, a furlong refers to a large group of parallel cultivated strips that would be equivalent in size to a very large field today.

Geophysical surveying of the Roman enclosures (near the A415 road) in Ham Field has revealed the faint outlines of earlier strip ploughing. The photograph also shows slight curves to the plough marks as they approach the headland, indicating that the marks could relate back to the use of oxen. It took such a distance to turn an ox-and-plough team around at the end of the strip being ploughed that there was a tendency to begin the turn before reaching the end of the strip, thus forming an elongated 'S' shape to the whole strip being cultivated.

During the early part of the Anglo-Saxon era the strip system would have been in its infancy with only small areas under cultivation close to the village. The area cultivated would have expanded slowly over several centuries as the population grew steadily throughout the Middle Ages.

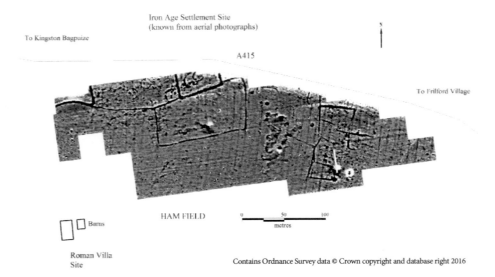

Iron Age Settlement Site
(known from aerial photographs)

To Kingston Bagpuize

A415

To Frilford Village

HAM FIELD

Barns

Roman Villa
Site

0        50       100
        metres

*Two geophysical survey images showing Romano-British enclosures and the outlines of early strip cultivation plough marks made by ox teams.*

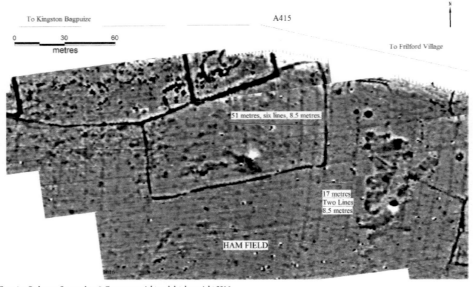

To Kingston Bagpuize

A415

To Frilford Village

0        30       60
        metres

51 metres, six lines, 8.5 metres.

17 metres
Two Lines
8.5 metres

HAM FIELD

**Images** (page 16)

The images on page 16 are recent geophysical surveys carried out by William Wintle in 2007, as part of his research into Roman villa sites in the Vale of the White Horse.

The top image clearly shows the ditch lines of Roman enclosures; in addition faint, curved lines indicating the position of medieval ploughing are a fascinating bonus, as they are the unseen evidence of the strips shown on the Enclosure Award map.

The bottom image is an enlargement of part of the top image. Here William Wintle has calculated the width of two sections of strips. The lower measurement indicates a width of seventeen metres for two visible lines/strips and the upper measurement, covering six lines/strips, measures fifty metres. When converted to chains both equal approximately two and a half chains and thus are both possible contenders for being directly related to the probable original strip widths. One could argue that the plough marks could be very recent; but a geophysical survey carried out by the same person, using the same equipment on land at Collins Farm, did not show any such plough marks in a situation where the land has been ploughed to a much greater depth in recent years, thus erasing any earlier plough marks.

However, the two strips totalling seventeen metres wide are equivalent to eight and a half metres each, which equals 0.42 of a chain, which in turn is exactly equal to one pole width. Similarly, the six strips totalling fifty metres are equivalent to 8.33 metres each, which equals 0.41 of a chain, or one pole width. In both cases the individual medieval strip width is almost equal and is *much* wider than the single passage of the widest multi-furrow modern plough; so the plough marks shown are definitely 'ancient'.

## Settlement

We do not know exactly where the original hamlet nucleus was situated, as there are no written records or remains of buildings any earlier than the seventeenth century. We are left to assume that their early wooden-framed buildings perished long ago as successive buildings were erected on approximately the same sites. The only evidence available to us is through the range of artefacts found in the fields close to the village.

Collins Farm is situated on the western side of the present hamlet, with immediate access to some of the best soils in the parish, in what is termed West Field on the enclosure map. A very noticeable humped ridge leading westwards from the farm is the only remaining evidence of the broad headland that divided two extensive furlongs.

*The humped ridge on the farm's western boundary that was originally the headland between two furlongs (fields). This is where the early cultivators would have turned their ox team round to begin the next plough run down their strip.*

Knowing the position of this original furlong as shown on the map, it is also possible to identify the faint remains of a second furlong headland that also headed westwards from the farmyard. The land between these two furlong headlands is a level, light sandy loam that remains very easy to cultivate. This area is relatively rich in Roman pottery shards and coins. In addition a few Celtic coins have also been found to bear witness to the land's continued use from the time of Cunobelinus, king of the Catuvellauni from AD 10–40. (*See Map B.*)

Adding these localised finds to our knowledge of the Iron Age settlement half a mile to the west confirms the extensive area within the parish that must have been fully cleared of woodland for the grazing of livestock at least. Recent deep ploughing on the better soils near to the village has erased all crop marks that could have confirmed a wider community or scatter of earlier hut circles.

We can safely state that the arrival of the Anglo-Saxons in the Frilford area, in the sixth century and onwards, would have been no more than the revival of a community that had existed in the area for over 1,000 years. They would have found the land extensively cleared of woodland and cultivated in small enclosure pockets with larger areas used for 'free-range' or managed grazing of cattle and sheep.

Some of the land is so light and sandy that it can 'blow' if over-cultivated in dry spring conditions. One is tempted to compare early land clearance and use in Frilford with our knowledge of the 'slash and burn' disasters in the forest regions of South America. The cleared land would soon have lost its fragile fertility and soil structure, acquired over many centuries whilst in a woodland state, once it was cultivated in the wrong manner or overgrazed in dry weather. Both would have soon depleted the light loam of its limited organic reserves. This would have led to the need for further woodland clearance to provide fresh, fertile cropping ground. So, Frilford never had a large community, but one that was constantly moving to fresh areas within the parish as diminishing soil fertility moved them about the local landscape.

The advent of a three-crop rotation resulted from the Anglo-Saxon's better understanding of land management; thus this parish witnessed the revival of an already long history of land use.

Frilford's mid-nineteenth-century enclosure map was drawn up at the end of the era of open-field farming, by which time the three-course, or three-field, system had encompassed most of the land within the parish that was capable of being cultivated.

The map (*see Map A, page 9*) shows the three large fields – **West Field**, extending westwards to the boundary with the neighbouring parish of Fyfield; **South Field**, set out to the south of the village and extending to a boundary with the River Ock; and finally **Ham Field**, the field furthest away from the village and requiring nearly a mile's walk to it from the edge of the village. Whilst this far-flung field is a long way from the heart of the present community, it is the field that contained the Roman villa and its attendant enclosures. It is also the field closest to the earlier Iron Age settlement. (*See Map C, page 13.*) Thus there was a relocation of habitation at some unknown point – probably with the coming of the Anglo-Saxons. One could speculate that they did not choose to start a new settlement on either of the earlier Iron Age or Roman sites, both of which are very exposed to the prevailing south-west winds. The present hamlet nestles into a convenient dip in the landscape, sheltered from the prevailing wind and close to the Piling Brook – a much closer source of fresh water than either of the earlier sites enjoyed.

With the arrival of the Anglo-Saxons, are we witnessing the benefits from a fresh 'immigrant' community bringing in new ideas, making use of the existing cleared lands yet setting up their homes in a new, sheltered position, close to fresh water and conveniently close to the best parcels of soil in the parish? They were a further chapter in the evolution of the English countryside, a process which continues to this day. Their contribution to the existence and identity of the present parish of Frilford has left its mark with the continuity of an 'open field' landscape.

This landscape remained very largely unchanged for many centuries and would have looked very much the same up to the beginning of the eighteenth century when the earliest of the remaining stone corn barns, and their related farmhouses, were erected at the beginning of what is termed 'the golden age' of farming. During this century industrial development expanded enormously, drawing men and their families from the land into the towns and cities to work in the new factories throughout the Midlands and the North of England, so depleting the land of its workforce. However, at the same time a combination of innovations in crop production and animal husbandry, coupled to the enclosure of farmland for more intensive cropping and the grazing of livestock, led to a reduction of workers required to work on the land.

With increasing industrialisation in both the countryside and the cities, necessary improvements in the network of roads and the new canal systems were providing the means to convey heavy goods more easily about the country.

## Communications and Transport over the Centuries

The River Thames had become the most convenient means for people to move about within a landscape that remained heavily wooded until the early Bronze Age, when large areas of woodland were cleared both for cultivation and to provide wood to fire their furnaces. In addition to rivers the other early means of traversing the country was along higher ground or hillsides, where the tree canopy would have not been so dense and the ground underfoot drier than the lower marshy valley lands. Areas of unforested open downland – such as the nearby Berkshire Downs and its ancient trackway, the Ridgeway – became alternative routes for the movement of people, goods and livestock from place to place.

The arrival of the Romans led to a formalisation of some of these ancient trackways into roads and they built a substantial road network to connect their military bases and the developing towns; we know that a length of Roman road stretched south from Oxford crossing the River Ock at Frilford and headed towards Wantage. (*A338*)

Over the following centuries many more rough tracks were established between rural communities to become the basis of the network of roads we know today, linking villages to their local towns.

The present main roads within the parish, the A338 running north–south from Oxford to Wantage and the A415 running east–west from Abingdon towards Faringdon or to the nearby River Thames, provided the people of Frilford with their communications to the outside world.

Some of these roads changed their position over the centuries to accommodate changing local requirements, for example, when the original track had become impassible due to overuse, winter weather damage or the constant movement of livestock within the parish forced the route to deviate onto adjacent fresh ground.

With the dawn of the industrial age, in the eighteenth century, the development of canal systems across the county greatly improved the ability to move heavier and more bulky goods cheaply over long distances. Locally, the building of the Wilts and Berks Canal began in 1796 to be completed in 1810. The canal linked the Kennet and Avon Canal at Semington, near Melksham, to the River Thames at Abingdon. It remained commercially active until closed in 1914, its demise hastened by the earlier collapse of the important Stanley aqueduct over the River Marden. By this date it had lost most of its traffic to the nearby Great Western Railway line, which had been laid from Bristol to London in 1840. The irony being that the canal was used to convey materials for the construction of the railway line!

The local benefits from the canal and the railway are shown by the provision of building materials used in the village which had been conveyed to the area from the slate mines of Wales and the heavy pine beams needed for the corn barn and cottage construction timbers that had been imported from North America.

# 2

# FRILFORD'S FARMING HISTORY

It is assumed that Frilford was part of the grant of the Manor of Marcham by King Edgar to Abingdon Abbey in AD 965.

At the time of the Domesday survey in 1086, the parish was still held by the Abbey of Abingdon and was assessed at ten hides, which represents about 1,200 acres. At the time of its enclosure, in 1861, Frilford was recorded as being 1,185 acres; thus its size had changed very little over the intervening 800 years and we have no knowledge of any other boundary changes over the centuries.

Because the hamlet has always been a small part of the larger ecclesiastical parish of Marcham there is very little historical evidence of its own fortunes during these centuries.

At the dissolution of the monasteries in 1546 the lands of the Abbey of Abingdon were given to one William Boxe of London. Eventually the copyhold (tenanted) lands at Frilford passed into the hands of the Elwes family as part of the Manor of Marcham.

The first references to the ownership of farmland in Frilford can be found in the inventory of Thomas Collins dated 1695. An earlier member of the same family gave his name to what first became known as Collins Free, and thence, with time, it became Collins Farm. The inventory lists all his 'goods, chattles, cattle and credits; household stuffs and implements of household stuffs' as at 10 January 1692. It is a comprehensive list, which shows the small number of six cattle, one horse, one pig and eleven sheep. But he did own one cart, one set of harrows and one plough. He had corn in the ground to the value of £7 and corn in the barn to the value of £12 and eight shillings, which, if it had been wheat, was then valued at £7 and eleven shillings; this works out at about only one and three-quarter tonnes of corn. This modest level of stored winter corn indicates that he was a typical small farmer. These possessions are regarded as being an average for someone who lived on the proceeds of annual crop yields from his quota of strips in the common fields at a time when the system was still the norm for unenclosed open-land farming.

Frilford is a small hamlet; it has never had a church or school of its own nor any shops or other trade buildings. It remained a purely agricultural community in constant and close contact with cropping the land; hence there were a disproportional number of corn barns, most of which have now been converted into homes. I list these to show how the hamlet was so closely connected to the produce from the land by the profusion of its mainly late eighteenth- and nineteenth-century barns:

**Ham Field Barn** – This large early nineteenth-century stone barn lying out in the middle of Ham Field was converted into a house within the past twenty years.

**Cradle Farm Barn** – This stone barn and its outbuildings were converted into a house in the 1970s.

**Collins Farm Barns** – A total of five traditional and one modern barn survive. Two have been converted into homes, two continue to perform a farming function, and one is attached to the original farmhouse and is in domestic use, leaving the oldest barn on the farm as a part shell that has been converted into a wood store. The majority of this early barn had become derelict by the 1920s and was taken down to build a state-of-the-art stone piggery building in the early 1930s, erected on part of the footprint of the original barn.

*The finest and last corn barn to be built (circa 1875) at Collins Farm as seen in 1970, following the repurchase of the farm. Note the abandoned and overgrown nature of the surroundings.*

**Ex-Aldworth Estate farm buildings** – Two large stone barns, both of which have recently been converted into separate houses, together with a smaller barn and an attached range of outbuildings that now form another home.

**The Old Grange** – There is still a fine, small cruck-framed seventeenth-century stone barn standing near the house. Nearby is another cottage that had formerly been a small barn.

**Champs Folly** – This is a cottage formed out of the remains of a stone barn with its attendant courtyard.

**Beverley House** – In the grounds of the house stands a small timber-framed corn store standing up on staddle stones. Adjacent is a small stone barn with a Cotswold slate roof.

**Peads Farm** – A completely rebuilt and well-restored thatched stone barn converted into a house in the 1980s.

*The oldest remaining barn in Frilford at the Old Grange. Although somewhat altered externally, it still has its original cruck timber framework that dates back to the seventeenth century, part of which can be seen through the open loft doorway.*

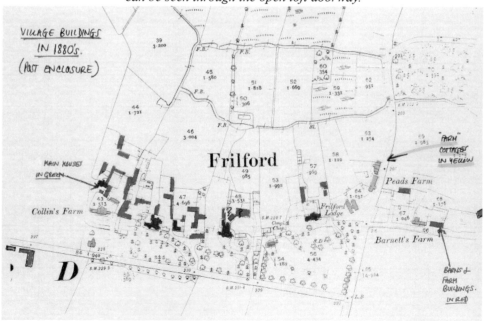

*The barns are coloured red, houses are green and cottages are yellow.*

**Barnett's Farm** – A large stone barn converted into a house in the 1980s. Further down the same (Ford) lane there are the remains of a barn, standing out in a field, that has been very derelict for well over half a century.

A total of seventeen corn barns in such a small parish hamlet, which comprised three fine large houses, four farmhouses and approximately eighteen workers' cottages, indicates that Frilford was an agricultural community first and foremost, relying on its neighbour Marcham for both its spiritual and its trade needs and to Garford for the local school. (*See map of Frilford village showing the barns, large houses and workers' cottages in the latter part of the nineteenth century.*)

Amongst my collection of artefacts found in the fields are parts of three sixteenth-to-eighteenth-century brass sheep bells, which indicate that flocks of sheep were present and played an important role in the farming rotation, helping to ensure the health and productivity of the main annual arable crops of wheat, barley and peas.

*The remnants of two sixteenth-to-eighteenth-century bell metal sheep bells found on the farm; many were made in Aldbourne, Wiltshire.*

When discussing the varying options for the rotation of crops in an open-field system, it is very easy to forget the very important role of sheep in the system. Their presence was vital to ensuring the health of the crops by carrying out three important functions. As they grazed across the post-harvest stubbles, or were winter-folded on crops of undersown turnips, their dung was returning valuable nutrients to the soil. If any land was left fallow for part of the year or as an annual break in the rotational crop cycle, the sheep would be folded on this ground to keep weed growth to a minimum.

Sheep would also graze land prior to ploughing to make it easier for the simple shallow draught ploughs to turn a clean furrow, so leaving the land visually clean and free of weeds prior to drilling the next crop.

Another use for sheep that is rarely mentioned was to fold them onto newly sown crops of winter barley or wheat for a very short period of time. Once the newly sown crop had become well established after drilling, the sheep would be introduced. They grazed the freshly emerged crop down for a very short spell, ensuring that they did not tear the young plants out of the ground; thus they would be allowed to graze off only part of the new growth. The crop would respond by producing a lot of tillers as it recovered, so growing a much denser crop; this thicker, well-tillered, regrowth was better able to compete with and smother out subsequent weed growth. It would have been a common practice for the women of the village to be sent out in early summer to pull out all obvious large, noxious perennial weeds, especially docks and thistles.

The Reverend Herbert Randolph was vicar of the adjacent parish of Marcham from 1819 and kept careful notes of all the tithes that were due to him from farmers in the three parishes that were within his ecclesiastical care.

Tithes due to him from Frilford are well recorded in these notes, and they throw a light on the number of sheep and their lambs owned and grazed on the parish fields. 'At Frilford nine hundred and eighty ewes, and seven hundred and seventy lambs belong to Messrs – T. Badcock, 400 ewes, 300 lambs; J. & T.

Aldworth, 240 ewes, 200 lambs; W. Badcock, 220 ewes, 180 lambs; T. Floyd, 120 ewes +.'

A stocking rate for sheep on poor ground is only about five per acre; thus the above number of sheep and their lambs would indicate that every tiny piece of fallow or stubble land in the three open fields, together with any summer meadows (after mowing for hay), would be grazed with folded sheep. Later in the autumn any old sheep and most ram lambs would be sold for slaughter. Other ewe lambs might be sold on to other local farmers to refresh their stocks. This would be necessary as there would not be enough grazing for all these sheep to eat once the grass stopped growing in late autumn.

The enclosure map for the parish shows that the cropping land was divided up into three large fields, indicating that a three-course rotation of crops had been practised for many centuries.

A tithe map, dated December 1850, states that the division of land in the parish fell into the following four categories:

725 acres as arable land,
98 acres as meadow and pasture,
345 acres as common field land and
31 acres as roads and waste.

Assuming that the 725 acres of arable land refers to the sum total of the three-field system, I have apportioned this as follows: 170 acres in West Field (all the land relating to Thomas Floyd, the farmer owning Collins Farm at the time, is within this block); 200 acres in South Field (a large part of this land was held by John Aldworth, the farmer owning Manor Farm, who was the only other signatory to the parish's Enclosure Act in 1861); and he also held land in the third field of 355 acres, approximately, in Ham Field. This field contains large areas of boggy springs, which slowly drain south to the River Ock.

From the information that has been outlined above, we know that the parish consisted of nearly 1,200 acres, of which 345 were common land, implying that this land was not fit to be cultivated as part of the three-crop rotation. This leaves the 725 acres to be split into the three cropping fields, as outlined above. We have a record of 150 acres of turnips, and the Reverend Randolph also states that 'there are many acres of clover for seed and to feed, early peas are extensively cultivated. There is thirty (acres) of mowing grounds. This year three hundred acres are sown to wheat.'

All the above could further reduce the area for cereal cropping, down to possibly only 650 acres. With 300 acres sown to wheat, we are left with the possibility that the one-year-in-three fallow took up the remaining acreage.

The existence of a large number of corn barns in the parish has been mentioned; but we do not know the average crop yield levels, except that the universally light dry soils of the parish would, and still do, not naturally provide high grain yields. The crops would have been stored in the barns in sheaf form to be hand-threshed with flails during the following winter and spring months, until the advent of the steam-powered threshing machines in the mid nineteenth century.

Most of the barns faced south so that their pairs of doors, in the centre of the north and south sides of the barn, could be opened on dry breezy days to allow the sheaves to be threshed on the wooden floor laid in the middle of the barn between the opposing doors. All the light and dusty chaff husks would be blow away and out of the barn by the prevailing southerly wind. With the advent of the steam-driven threshing machine, it would have stood in this same place, inside the barn between the opposing pairs of doors.

In 1809, William Mavor was commissioned by the Board of Agriculture, in London, to produce his book *A General View of the Agriculture of Berkshire*. In the chapter dealing with the rotation of crops he makes the following observation:

**Kingston Bagpuize**. A light sandy soil. Wheat on grass leys – Peas – Barley – part of the field is always in turnips or sown grass – the fallow preceding the wheat always produces a green crop of some kind. Being unenclosed the field is thrown into four quarters.

*The view into the partly derelict Ham Field Barn (since converted into a dwelling) well illustrates the layout of corn barns to facilitate the threshing of the sheaves stored within. The open central section allows for a good through draught to blow away the chaff and dust generated by the process of either hand-flail or machine threshing.*

I interpret this to indicate that this neighbouring parish had by this date progressed to a four-course rotation sequence of a grass or green fallow crop followed by wheat, then peas or beans, and finally barley, after which the sequence would repeat itself. The (first year) green fallow crop and the (third year) crop of peas or beans would have maintained the fertility of the land for the other two more valuable crops of wheat and barley.

Mavor also reports on the cropping in Marcham:

> Soil light sand, stone brash, and some clay and peat. 1. Barley with seeds; 2. Green crop; 3. Wheat; 4. Barley, with seeds, &c.; so that wheat is grown once in four years: or, 1. Wheat; 2. Barley, with seeds, and one part fallow for turnips; 3. Peas, or some beans; 4. Barley.

Again a four-course rotation had developed by the nineteenth century in this neighbouring parish as well. With so many

31

nineteenth-century-built corn barns in Frilford, I feel that this parish may have continued to try and earn more from the two valuable corn crops with its original three-course rotation remaining in operation longer than its neighbouring parishes.

For earlier information on the cropping of local parish lands, we are fortunate in being able to refer to the detailed farm diaries of Robert Loder, who farmed nearby, at Harwell. He had recorded in great detail his farm crops and accounts for the period 1610 to 1620.

At that time Harwell was an open-field parish with arable cropping in two large fields and pasture rights in three other areas, making for a possible three-course rotation. The crops grown are similar to those recorded (see above) by William Mavor two centuries later, being grown at Kingston Bagpuize and Marcham. One is justified in assuming that the range of crops grown in Frilford would have been similar to those of its neighbouring parishes.

It is also possible that there may have been fewer changes to the original crop rotations in Frilford whilst this parish remained unenclosed, with its three very distinctive fields, and thus it possibly remained restricted to the original cropping pattern and rules laid down many centuries earlier by the manorial court for each parish within the manor.

The Reverend Herbert Randolph, vicar of Marcham, in 1819 records:

Frilford consists of eleven hundred and twenty acres, four hundred being common, the tithe of the Furze [gorse] on which is of great value.
    One hundred and fifty acres of turneps are grown at Frilford.
The number of cows kept at Frilford is twenty four.

The amount of turnips grown indicates that there were a lot of sheep to be folded and fed through the winter months, especially when one takes into account that all the summer's corn crop stubbles would be available as well for winter grazing.

The furze, or gorse, would have been in the north of the parish, in the area now covered by the golf club, extending up to Tubney Woods and eastwards to the present Sheepstead Farm – a large area, where it is still to be found.

The small number of cows indicates that they were only kept as 'house cows', to provide milk for the farmers' families. They had no means of keeping milk fresh enough for transporting to Abingdon or Oxford to be sold.

# 3

# FRILFORD'S PARISH ENCLOSURE

The enclosure movement was the process which ended the traditional manorial rights of the villagers (commoners), small farmers and tenants to have access to all the areas of common land, meadows and waste land within the parish as well as their entitlement to individually nominated strips of cropping land in each of the three large fields within the parish's open-field system.

The strips were often about 220 yards, or one furlong, in length and varied in width in units of about 5.5 yards, equivalent to one pole – pole, rod and perch are different names for the same unit of measurement. (*See Maps B and C, plus images on page 16 with their explanatory notes on page 17.*)

The strips were originally allocated so that each household in the parish eligible for cropping land was given an equal amount of both the bad and good ground. They all knew which were the areas of good, fertile land and likewise did not want any more of the poor land than a neighbour! Thus each farming household had numerous strips of ground dotted about in each of the three fields, which made cultivations very time-consuming as they moved from one small strip to another to cultivate, sow or harvest their crops.

Once the parish fields were enclosed, these open areas and strip allocations ceased to exist and the land was fenced or hedged and deeded to one or more larger, individual farmers within the parish. Thus many of the villagers lost all their rights of access to the parish's former common and waste land. Other smaller farmers were allocated such limited areas that they did not have adequate land to make a living; so they were forced to sell their allocation to a neighbour who had been granted a larger share.

The enclosures during the eighteenth and nineteenth centuries were made by means of local Acts of Parliament and called the Enclosure Acts. These separate parish Acts consolidated the individual's scattered strips in the open fields into compact farm units, which could now be managed independently by the new landowner. All the other parish commons and waste land were treated in a similar fashion and passed to an adjoining landowner to add to his other consolidated allocation of cropping land.

In many parishes the poorest villagers were thus forced to leave the land and seek employment in a nearby town or factory. Because Frilford had such a small village population it is likely that the few remaining poorer 'commoners' sought employment with one or other of the remaining larger farmers, who would have needed more staff to be able to manage their extra land effectively.

In the mid eighteenth century, well prior to enclosure, we have a record of twelve 'proprietors' – small farmers in the parish signing an agreement, dated June 1735, whereby they all agreed to give up small pieces of their land to form access tracks into several meadows for their communal use at haymaking time. So we know that by this date there were at least twelve individual farmers with rights to land in the parish fields.

By the time of the first attempt at an Enclosure Act, a century later, in 1846 there were only three farmers' names recorded on the draft document, from which we must assume that most of the descendants of those small farmers in the previous century had given up their allocation of strips, passing them on to the remaining larger strip holders, who would most likely have been allowed to consolidate their former narrow individual strips into larger blocks of cropping land.

By the time the Enclosure Act was finally agreed and passed

in 1861 there were only two major landholders' names recorded as signatories to the agreement: those of John Aldworth and Thomas Floyd. There is no record of why the original attempt to pass an Enclosure Act, in 1846, was not implemented until fifteen years later. Both of the two final signatories were listed on the earlier attempted agreement. It is the latter of the two who was the owner of Collins Farm and who was not deterred from carrying out considerable farm improvements following the failure of the original draft agreement.

# 4

# THE FARMERS AT COLLINS FARM

## Following Enclosure

Thomas Floyd had been farming at Collins Farm prior to the initial attempt at enclosure, but the failure to reach an agreement in 1846 did not deter him from embarking on an impressive modernisation of the farm buildings. He had already built a new stone corn barn with one of its main beams dated 1844. With the neighbouring parishes enclosed, he must have realised that the Act would have to be passed at some point in the near future because most of the other villages in the Vale of the White Horse had been enclosed for some time. He would have noted that enclosure had allowed those remaining farmers to expand and modernise their crop production and to reduce costs, leading to increased profitability, of which he wished to take advantage.

Thus Thomas Floyd embarked on building new cottages and another barn. The building of one foreman's two-bedroom cottage in 1854 was shortly followed by a block of three workers' cottages, with a communal toilet in the garden and a central bread oven to serve all three cottages.

A new corn barn was erected the following year adjacent to the farmhouse with its main beam dated 1855. This was a major investment in both farming and social terms. It also shows his confidence in the future of farming and in his growing family. His son, also named Thomas, born in 1846, was to take over the title of the farm five years after the death of his father, aged seventy-one, in 1863. The younger Thomas would have been only twenty-two years old at the time of his father's death, but would have had the support of his mother and his older sister, Martha. The young man is not recorded as living at home at the time of the 1861 census, just before the death of his father; so he was either away at school or as an apprentice on another farm.

*The block of three cottages built by Thomas Floyd in 1854, for his farm staff. Already two have been converted into one in this photo taken in 2000. At either end are outhouses for storage use. A communal bread oven was situated in a small extension at the rear of the cottages.*

The younger Thomas married Elisabeth (surname unknown) at the age of twenty-five in about 1872, as they are recorded as having a son, another Thomas, aged eight, and a daughter, Ethel, aged four, at the time of the 1881 census. He followed his father's example by being a progressive farmer and built the last of the traditional corn barns on the farm before 1875; this barn is undated. He remained at Collins Farm until selling the farm in 1894. Thus the Floyd family's connection with the land had extended over a period of nearly fifty productive years. The material benefits of their ownership remain to this day with a compact, well-built set of farm buildings and a fine hawthorn hedge planted as a requirement of the enclosure agreement. This hedge continues to provide good wind protection 150 years later.

Their farming fortunes would have fluctuated over the years as is common with many businesses, especially those reliant upon fickle markets and the weather.

The price of cereals fluctuated from year to year dependent on weather and harvest conditions; but in 1875 the first shipments of grain and chilled beef came into the country from America and heralded the onset of a depression for home-grown agricultural commodity prices that did not recover until the advent of the First World War.

The national census held every ten years throws a little light on the possible fluctuations of their farming fortunes. The census of 1851, soon after the Floyd family's arrival at Collins Farm, lists them as employing ten men. By the 1861 census they are recorded employing twenty-five men, women and boys. There is no breakdown of this total, but I expect that the women would have been the wives of the full-time employed men and would have worked part-time stone-picking in the fields, pulling weeds during the growing season and then helping with the harvest. Likewise the boys would be out bird-scaring, leading in the horses at harvest time and doing other simple chores; they would have all been members of the same working families, helping to ensure enough income to buy adequate food and clothing for the family.

The 1871 census is a little more informative in that it states that the Floyds were employing seventeen men and four boys on 333 acres of arable crops and dairy. This latter reference to dairy production indicates that they may have reduced their cereal production as corn prices began to fall and, with the arrival of the Great Western Railway into the Vale in the 1840s, they could have taken their milk to Wantage Road Station for delivery to meet the growing demand in London. There is still the original small stone dairy building on the farm with stalls for five cattle.

The cobbled floor with its brick drainage channel and stone feeding trough is still in good order.

By 1881, the farm was employing eighteen men, five boys and five women on 348 acres of land. No references in this census to cropping details. With more wheat and beef now coming into the country from America it is most likely that they had maintained their milk production and would have needed all the hay that their access to the water meadows could provide to feed the cattle through the winter months, which the light sandy arable land could not produce. They would have grown some winter barley to provide supplementary feed for the dairy cattle; thus the corn barns remained key buildings to store both the hay and sheaves of corn.

The 1891 census gives little information of interest. By then Thomas Floyd senior was forty-five and their son (again called Thomas) was eighteen; but in 1894, when his son would have been twenty-one and ready to become involved in the farm, the family sold the farm to Gerald Phillips. We do not know the reason for their decision to sell at a time when the son was old enough to take on a responsible position alongside his forty-eight-year-old father. It could have been a response to the two severe drought years of 1892 and 1893, with the price of wheat continuing to fall regardless of the poor harvests, or simply a decision by the younger Thomas not wishing to follow in his father's footsteps.

(As I write these words I am faced with a similar dilemma: my son has built up his own thriving tree-surgery business based at the farm and does not wish to take on the mantle of farming the land. I have passed the normal age of retirement, but, like many older farmers today, I will continue to farm at a more relaxed pace for the foreseeable future, pending a solution being found to retain the working farm in the family.)

There are no current records of what became of the Floyd family after the sale, except that they moved to nearby Longworth and became actively involved in that community.

The 1901 census shows Mr Gerald Phillips, aged thirty-one, as being the owner of the farm, but not living in the village, his home then being in Chieveley.

**Mr. G. E. Phillips.**

*Gerald Phillips, the gentleman owner of Collins Farm
from 1894 until his death in 1936.*

He is recorded in the 1911 census as living in the parish at
Frilford Lodge (now Beverley House). He continued to own the
farm until he died in 1936, at the age of sixty-six. There is no
record of how he farmed the land, but a Ministry of Agriculture
return for the period 1910/12 shows him as the owner and the
farm occupied by William Woodley, probably as his tenant.

He made a major investment in the construction of a state
-of-the-art Danish-type pig-fattening house. This building was
constructed and attached to the back of the most recent corn
barn. It stands on part of the footprint of what had been the oldest
barn on the farm, which had become derelict. He took down most
of this barn and used the stone to build the low walls of this new
building, which has a very low-pitch timber-framed roof, lined
on the inside with close wood boarding and the roof clad on the
top with corrugated tin sheeting. There is an open, ventilated,
apex to the roof and further ventilation between the inner roof

41

boarding and the outer tin sheeting; both being key elements of the building's design to provide the necessary warmth, light and ventilation for the high density of pigs to be housed within.

*The pig building erected by Gerald Phillips in about 1930, with its ventilated low-pitch roof, originally clad with corrugated tin sheet, now re-clad with a new tin roof and an overhang added to act as a machinery shelter. In the background can be seen the remains of the oldest stone barn, now an open-fronted store.*

Inside the piggery was a central feeding passageway with pens on either side. The Crittal metal windows, along each side of the building, not only provide light but are positioned low so that, when cleaning out the pens, the manure could be thrown out of the top half of the windows, which are removable!

A Ministry of Agriculture bulletin on pig keeping, first published in 1925, shows pictures of very similar buildings. I feel that this building was put up at about the same time, when prices for agricultural products had revived after the depressed period following the First World War. Prices were quite buoyant during the period from 1925 to 1931, after which they declined again until the advent of the Second World War. All businesses need some form of stimulus to invest. With the absence of government grant aid, the response could have been the prospect of a brighter future offered by improved market prices.

The Sprackman family had arrived in Frilford with the purchase of the nearby Manor Farm in 1931. When Mr Phillips decided to sell Collins Farm in 1936 they bought it to extend their farming operations. During the war years Mr Sprackman's brother-in-law moved up from Kent to get away from the bombing and took on the running of Collins Farm until returning to Kent at the end of the war.

The family farmed in the parish until selling up in 1946 to move back down to a large family farm near Bristol. All the following information about the family's time in Frilford was given to me by Mr Sprackman's son, who was a teenager at the time. He still farms at Bristol, with his son now largely in charge of daily work.

I have been able to verify a lot of what his son told me by seeing, and being able to photocopy, their Ministry of Agriculture Return of their farming operations for the year 1941, covering the two farms. These records are held in the Public Records Office at Kew.

The crops listed included forty-two acres of wheat, thirty-three acres of barley, fifty-two acres of oats, eleven acres of mixed corn, one and a half acres of potatoes, two acres of fodder turnips, three acres of mangolds, one acre of carrots, fifteen acres of clover, eighty-two acres of grass for mowing, and thirty-two and a half acres of permanent grass.

The list of livestock read as follows: one bull, twenty calves, twenty cows, forty bull calves for rearing, one ram, fifty breeding ewes, 251 other sheep over one year old, seventy other sheep under one year old, ninety poultry and two horses (one mare and one gelding).

The diversity of crops and the wider range of livestock listed above were common to many farms at that time, unlike the near mono-cropping, and absence of any livestock, on many farms today.

In addition to the lists of crops and livestock on the MAFF Return, there are added comments on the condition of the farm –

its buildings, roads, fences, ditches and drainage. These comments were added by a visiting agriculture inspector. In most cases a 'fair' condition was recorded, which ties up with their admission of trying to make a profit by not spending unnecessarily. Farming had been through lean times in the run-up to the beginning of the Second World War and farmers had learnt to be frugal to survive. The good times were yet to come.

During their time in the parish they farmed frugally. Few improvements were made to the buildings and maintenance was kept to a minimum. The oldest building on the farm, probably dating back to the seventeenth century, is a small, narrow, thick-stone-walled structure that is now a single-storey farm office. We know that during the wartime it had been a double-storey building with a pigeon loft in the upper part, under a red tiled roof. Assuming that the pigeon nest holes were constructed into the upper wall, as was common for all such stone lofts, one suspects that the roof had fallen into disrepair and the upper walls likewise had become unstable, with the pigeon nest holes reducing the strength of the wall to the point where it was decided to take down the upper storey and put on a simple single-slope tin roof to reduce the building to its present height. Historically such a building would have housed a piggery on the lower ground floor, which is evident from a number of large openings along three sides, to provide plenty of ventilation. All these openings are now glazed to give light into the offices.

The Sprackmans concentrated on rearing cattle, purchasing Irish store cattle from a dealer at Bristol docks. The cattle were transported up to the farm; on occasions the family would awake to find the new arrivals safely deposited in the open cattle yard and the lorry long gone!

The relatively new special pig building and most other small buildings were used to house their store cattle and raise heifers. I have a copy of his daybook during their time here, in which he recorded all the cattle movements and sales. It shows that they were actively trading in cattle, sheep and pigs, which they had raised either indoors or out on the light land pastures. They sold the cattle locally or took them to market in Abingdon. There is a verbal record of some cattle being driven along the road to Grove Station, where they were entrained to their new destination.

*End view of the oldest building on the farm, which was originally a*
*piggery with a pigeon loft above, now missing. With the upper storey*
*removed during the Second World War it was left as a near-flat-roofed*
*chicken shed until we built up the walls to take a gently sloping slate*
*roof to form the present-day farm offices.*

They grew winter-sown oats and barley, the latter being the
popular short-strawed variety Spratt Archer, which was strong
and stood well, yielding high grain quality. The crop was cut
with their six-foot-cut Massey-Harris binder drawn by one of
the tractors. The sheaves were stacked in two large ricks situated
in the middle of the farm, as well as other smaller ricks in the
farmyard. The ricks were placed beside each other, in pairs, so that
their Ransomes threshing machine could be positioned between
the two ricks to be able to thresh both without the need to move
the machine and its attendant stationary Powell baler. There is
an interesting invoice from Messrs White & Sons, agricultural
engineers and smiths, of Appleton. The account covers the period
from December 1942 to June 1943 for the supply of baling wire
and repairs to both the threshing machine and the baler. The
bill was not paid until mid January 1944! – it was common for
many farmers not to settle their accounts with local traders until
well after harvest, when they would have received income from
the sales of corn and livestock sold before the onset of winter.

The winter oats variety Aberystwyth S 147 was grown to make up their cattle rations, with any crop surplus being sold on. One surviving account from Harris & Matthews of Abingdon, dated September–October 1945, lists their purchase of both barley and feed oats.

Mains electricity and water had been brought to the farm by 1941, yet some water on the farm continued to be drawn from a number of wells around the farmyard, as was common at the time across the country.

The Sprackmans were early users of tractors, only keeping two carthorses for doing light work, such as feeding stock, hoeing the root crops or carting small loads of hay or straw around the farm to feed outdoor livestock. Most cultivations were done by their Standard Fordson and International 10/20 tractors. They had a shepherd's hut on wheels that was either out in the field with their cross-bred tegs or it stood in the main yard – in the same place where a restored old Lincolnshire shepherd's hut now stands!

*This shepherd's hut was rescued from a local farm and restored by us.*
*It is identical to one used by a neighbouring farmer who continued*
*to fold his sheep in West Field until the 1970s and is likely to be of a*
*similar pattern to the one used by the Sprackmans in the 1940s.*

## Frilford in Wartime

At this point I wish to pause with the farming history of the parish to explain how the landscape of Frilford was altered by events during the Second World War.

*The 28A-type pillbox shown is on the edge of the field adjacent, and very close, to the one on Collins Farm. This one remains unaltered and shows the wide embrasure for the two-pounder gun with the entrance showing behind. The thickness of the reinforced concrete is very visible. The side walls are equally substantial.*

With the fall of France and the evacuation from Dunkirk in June 1940, General Ironside was given the task of preparing coastal and inland defences with the expectation of a German invasion. In under eight weeks he had set in motion the most extensive lines of fortification yet constructed to prevent German troops penetrating England's heartland. One of these local fortified lines was a stretch of anti-tank ditch, coupled to concrete pillboxes placed along the ditch line, to deal with enemy tanks trying to cross the deep and wide trench. Called the Red Line, this stretch of the anti-tank ditch ran from the Thames at Newbridge, across Appleton Common to Fyfield, on to Frilford and Marcham, crossing Abingdon Common to join the Thames at Abingdon.

This particular short stretch of the Red Line was designed to stop the enemy approaches to Oxford. The defensive line was manned by the local Home Guard units during the war. I have a very detailed, and rare, operations map of this section of the line showing who was guarding it and the munitions available to them.

The pillboxes on this stretch of line were mostly of the 28A type designed to accommodate a two-pounder anti-tank gun. The guns would have only been put in place at the last moment; they were in the controlling hands of local regular army units.

The local Home Guard units were mostly issued with First World War Lee–Enfield rifles and live ammunition. The odd Lewis gun, mortar or Bren machine gun was available along the line. We have found spent .303 cartridge cases and a few badges relating to the presence of the Home Guard during this period.

The aerial reconnaissance photo taken in March 1944 shows the trench crossing the fields from Fyfield and proceeding diagonally across Collins Farm to a roadblock on the main road, thence along the southern side of the village towards Marcham.

A large slice of the farm was isolated, making access and cropping of those fields difficult. The trench was filled in at the end of the war, but its mark remained visible for many years where the soil had been poorly replaced. Where the trench had been cut through patches of the limestone brash, a lot of stones are very visible and still make cultivations difficult in these areas.

Nearly all the substantially built, thick concrete pillboxes still remain along the trench line and Collins Farm has one close to its western hedge boundary. We have enclosed all the rifle slits and the larger opening where the two-pounder gun would have been positioned. With double doors on the back of the pillbox, it now serves as a safe shelter for small machinery and a very secure farm chemical store. Adjacent to this pillbox we excavated a stretch of the original anti-tank trench to show its depth and width, which would have been an impressive obstacle to cross, being approximately eight feet deep and twelve feet wide at the top. All the spoil from digging out the trench was piled up on each side to make it even harder for a tank to cross.

*An aerial survey photo taken on 8 March 1944, showing the line of the anti-tank trench and the pair of protecting pillboxes, in the centre of the photo, at the juncture where the trench changes direction to head south across Collins Farm to meet the main road (A415). There were several large concrete roadblocks at the point where it crossed the road.*

*The outline of the anti-tank trench shows up as weed growth as it crosses a stubble field on Collins Farm. The pillboxes are beside the group of tall poplar trees on the horizon beyond the tractor ploughing the field.*

*A view along the short stretch of the anti-tank trench that we excavated some years ago. Originally all the soil dug out of the trench was piled up along both sides of the trench to further deepen the trench, making it a difficult obstacle to be overcome.*

*Artefacts found on the farm relating to the presence of both the Home Guard and troops billeted on the farm in the run-up to D-Day. A Pioneer Corps cap badge, a Home Guard badge and a couple of .303 cartridges.*

In the build-up to the D-Day landings, units of American and Polish forces were billeted under canvas in the village. US servicemen camped in tents erected in the shade of large elm trees that lined the west side of the paddock below the farm buildings. Huts were also erected in this paddock – an oval brass tag, inscribed 'Hut 3' on one side and with 'Perry- W D- P' on the other, was found, along with a Pioneer Corps cap badge. Their presence has confirmed camping in this area whilst building quarters for other servicemen in the village. A large stone corn barn down the next lane was used as a mess hall for the troops, with the kitchens in the buildings behind. A painted wooden door with the faint white-paint imprint, in Polish, of 'Cookhouse' survived the recent conversion of these farm buildings and is in the possession of the owner. Nearby a derelict cottage was converted into a washroom. One or two huts still remain in the village and are now used for general storage.

One of the farm cottages on Collins Farm was occupied by the

Bolton family. Their son was a teenager at the time and helped with some part-time work on the farm for the Sprackmans. He recounts a couple of wartime incidents that he witnessed. A small military glider landed near the main track that led up the middle of the farm. Service personnel arrived, unbolted the wings and then simply wheeled it away to a transporter.

Later in the war Winston Churchill came to inspect a large number of US servicemen who paraded for him in the large field just beyond the farm's long hawthorn hedge on the western boundary. The same aerial reconnaissance photo, taken in March 1944, shows some hard-to-define non-farming activity in the same field. (*See page 49.*)

The Home Guard practised firing their mortar from near the main road, firing northwards up the line of the anti-tank ditch. This was confirmed by the discovery of a live mortar shell whilst we were harvesting potatoes in the 1980s. The local policeman called in the bomb disposal unit, who detonated the shell on the farm because it was too unstable to be taken away. I have part of the fuse cap in my little farm museum.

With D-Day passed and the Allies moving across France, all threats of a German invasion were now in the past and even the Sprackmans were looking to the future. In early July 1944 Mr Sprackman wrote to the Berkshire War Agricultural Committee, who had been in charge of farming and food production targets within the county, to ask them if they would leave the concrete pillbox on the farm, saying:

> There is a pillbox, which was built near the tank trap. If it would save you the trouble of moving it, you could leave it, as it is not in the way and it may be useful to put a tractor in at any time. Of course I should not be prepared to pay anything; but thought it may save you the expense of moving it –
> Yrs E. W. Sprackman.

These pillboxes were so substantially built that very few have subsequently been demolished. Early post-war attempts to blow up and remove a few large bunkers on Kingston Hill were abandoned and remain as a large pile of twisted metal and broken concrete, too expensive to justify their complete removal!

## Post-War at Collins Farm

Following the end of the war the Sprackman family decided to move back to Bristol. They put the farm on the market and sold it to Harold Froude, who was the owner of the 'rough' Noah's Ark pub in the hamlet near the River Ock and beside the road to Wantage. Here he also milked a small herd of cows.

*Harold Froude at the wheel of his converted Morris Commercial pickup with Jack Walters standing beside it. The dirty state of the back of the vehicle would indicate they had been carting manure. Note the overgrown nature of the meadow with large patches of nettles, etc., – a sure sign of subsistence farming.*

He ran the farm for only three years, taking on casual staff to help him at haymaking and harvest times. There is a photo of him at the wheel of a converted Morris Commercial lorry being used to cart slurry, by the look of what had been its load. Standing beside him is Jack Walters, who lived his whole life in the village. At the time Jack was a young man and was obviously helping out on a summer's day.

There is another photo of the main farmyard showing a quantity of chickens, ducks and the odd turkey that appear to be free-range in the yard!

There is no record of why Harold Froude sold up after such a short time.

*The farmyard (1946–9) showing an assortment of free-range chickens, ducks and the odd turkey. Behind can be seen the corn barn with its open doors. To the left is a range of wooden pigsties, which had become completely dilapidated by the time we repurchased the farm in 1969 and were cleared away to provide the site for a new cold store a few years later. Behind the pigsties can be seen the remaining walls of the derelict barn that had been partly demolished earlier to build the walls of the new piggery situated behind the corn barn. On the left in the background are several large elm trees, under which the American servicemen had camped in their tents prior to D-Day.*

In 1949 the farm passed into the possession of John Povey, who owned it for ten years until selling it to my father in 1959. Once again we have little information about how Mr Povey farmed except that he kept a large number of outdoor pigs, for which the light sandy land would have been ideal. He is likely to have made full use of the purpose-built piggery and a range of wooden pigsties that appear in the photo of the farmyard taken a few years before.

However, we do have tangible evidence about his ability to do a good job from a number of Drayton and District Farming Club crop competition award cards that are pinned to a barn wall. I covered them over many years ago to preserve them.

In 1952 he won a '1st in class' award for '3 acres of Spring Barley'; in 1953 he won a '1st in class' award for 'Best acre of Fodder Beet'; and again in 1955 he won a '1st in class' award for '3 acres of Oats' and '2nd in class' awards for 'Best acre of Fodder Beet' and 'Best 3 acres of Spring Wheat'. These awards show that he was doing a good job and that he was growing a wide range of crops, probably using most of it as animal feed for his livestock.

From the few photos and our knowledge of the state of the farm when we first bought it in 1959, it is safe to say that the buildings and farmyard had remained neglected since before the war. Fortunately, the majority of the fine nineteenth-century stone barns had been well built originally and so had continued to do their job with minimum maintenance. The only noticeable repair work that had been done to two of the biggest stone barns was the construction of buttresses to support walls that had begun to subside and so lean outwards. This was due to inadequate foundations when they were first built in the mid nineteenth century.

*Another farmyard scene during the same period showing two farmhands repairing the door to the cart shed behind. Today we park our car in this building. The old tin has been replaced by timber cladding and the flimsy doors are long gone! Behind can be seen the end of the farmhouse in the distance and on the right another corn barn, still with its Stonesfield slate roof. This barn has since been converted into a dwelling.*

# 5

# ALL CHANGE: THE ARRIVAL OF HORTICULTURE AT FRILFORD

My involvement in the evolution and history of land use in Frilford began with a decision upon leaving school in the summer of 1959.

I decided to join my father fruit-growing on his farm in the neighbouring parish of Kingston Bagpuize. He was pleased that I had made such a decision, but said that his farm was not big enough to be able to absorb me into the existing business; so we agreed to look for more land in the locality to be able start up a new orchard that I would eventually manage on my return from a course in general horticulture at what is now called Writtle College, near Chelmsford in Essex.

It was a requirement of entry to the course that one spent a year working on a suitable farm prior to going to the college. I was allowed to do my year's practical on my father's farm because he was pioneering a new system of growing apples and pears. To describe the new approach simply, the trees in most modern fruit orchards by the late 1950s were grown as a low bush form, which had largely replaced earlier generations of widely planted half-standard or full-standard trees. Father had developed a tree form that he called 'The Pillar System', whereby the closely planted rows of trees consisted of a single trunk, no more than three metres tall, with the crop carried on a three-year rotation of young, short branches growing out from the main stem. It was a very simple system to master and made the work of managing the tree throughout the year much easier than all previous tree forms. His system has since been superseded by a wide range of densely planted single-stem, staked tree forms.

*My father looking at my pruning of the maturing Pillar System apple trees in about 1968. The trees have reached their final height. We kept the overall height to no more than twelve feet (3.5 m) so that the fruit could be picked using only a short, three-step, tripod ladder. The orchard had been grassed down with grass between the trees, to help control the vigorous tree growth.*

He was fortunate to see an advertisement for the sale of a small seventy-six-acre farm on the western side of the small hamlet of Frilford. The owner had been growing a traditional range of agricultural crops and producing pigs. The purchase was completed in the summer of 1959.

My father quickly decided that he did not need all the acreage that he had bought for his proposed new orchard; so he chose to keep only the two most westerly fields, about twenty-two acres in total, and the set of farm cottages. These two fields were bounded by a stream along their northern boundary and the main road (A415) along the southern boundary. The stream was to play a very important part in the future profitability of the venture.

The rest of the farm was then put back on the market as a smaller unit, but still containing all the main farm buildings and farmhouse with an adjacent compact block of land. This was sold by the following spring to Marshall Bowey from Abingdon, who had limited experience of dairy farming which he planned to do. In the meantime we got to work to tidy up the land to be sold and to dispose of the stored grain. The harvest of oats had to be bagged up by hand into the then familiar large hessian grain sacks and loaded onto a lorry for dispatch – warm work on a winter's day.

The land that he had chosen to retain was typical of all the soils in the parish, a light sandy limestone soil overlying outcrops of limestone brash that came within thirty centimetres of the surface in patches. The shallow depth of workable soil was to prove a problem when we came to planting the fruit trees, as we had to crowbar holes through this platy limestone to get an adequate planting depth for some of the trees.

Throughout the early winter of 1959/60 I worked with one of Father's staff to fence around the two fields to keep out all rabbits and hares before we could begin to plant the fruit trees.

The planting of fruit trees began in January 1960 and continued until spring. The Pillar System of tree production is such that because of the way the trees are hard-pruned, with only a three-year cycle of young growth up the single stem, there is a tendency for the trees to produce very vigorous growth. The light brashy soil should have helped to minimise excessive tree growth. At the time of planting there was a new range of fruit-tree rootstocks available to growers, which influence both the growth rate and tree form. Growers would choose a rootstock suited to their soil type and to the tree form that they planned to plant.

Father was not familiar with the growth rate and cropping potential of this new range of rootstocks, so chose to experiment with five different rootstocks, only one of which he had any previous experience of growing. Over the coming years this choice was to be the deciding factor in the overall failure of the orchard to produce profitable crop yields. Only the one rootstock that he had previously used and one of the new range proved to be suited to the poor soil and hard-pruning regime.

I continued to work in both orchards until I went to college in the autumn for the year's course, returning to take up the management and completion of planting of the new Frilford orchard on my return in summer 1961.

During the following year we completed the orchard planting on most of the land at Frilford, with a small acreage of loganberries to fill the remaining ground.

In 1963 I began to rent other land locally to grow crops of sweetcorn, which at the time was a very new crop in England. I had got to know an American air-force major, who was in charge of the base shop and canteen at the nearby large USAAF airbase at Brize Norton. He had been unable to bring in supplies of fresh sweetcorn from the United States, so was keen for me to grow the crop under contract to supply their needs on the base. All subsequent deliveries of sweetcorn had to be taken to a quality-control centre, where each consignment was tested with a tenderometer to ensure that the cobs' kernels were both fresh and tender enough for the discerning palates of the servicemen and women.

We were aware of the poor moisture retention of the light coral rag limestone soil, so invested in portable aluminium irrigation equipment to be able to extract water from the small stream to irrigate the young trees. As the need for irrigation grew, we reached the point where the stream's flow rate in midsummer was no longer adequate to meet our water demands, so we hired a dragline excavator to dig out a big pond into the side of the stream. We then dammed the steam to hold back an adequate volume of water in the new pond to be able to irrigate more of the fruit trees.

We later heard that the local council planned to expand a water treatment plant upstream at Appleton, which would greatly increase the flow of available, cleaned, water throughout the whole year, but especially during the summer months. We installed a small temporary sluice in the stream to hold back some of this new excess water, enabling us to extract our needs direct from the stream, yet without stopping the overall water flow down the stream.

The ability to irrigate was to have a profound effect on the range of crops that we could grow and consequently the profitability of the farm in the years to come.

As the young orchard developed and began to produce crops, another problem with the site arose; half the orchard was planted on a north-facing slope running down to the stream and the belt of trees growing alongside. This produced the ideal conditions for a frost 'pocket' to form on cold spring nights, which would damage the fruit buds as they came into flower. The failure of the fruit trees in this area to produce a crop soon became evident. At the time there were two options to prevent frost damage: we could buy large burners which burnt waste oil or cleaner diesel fuel – these would have to be lit when the temperature dropped to freezing point and kept burning until the temperature rose above freezing again with the approach of dawn – or we could install an overhead frost-prevention irrigation system. We chose the latter.

The use of water to prevent frost damage works on the principle of the transfer of latent heat. When water freezes it gives up its heat to that with which it is in contact. Thus if one applies overhead water continuously to the fruit trees during a frost, ice will form around the fruit buds but the temperature will not drop lower than freezing point so long as water is being continually applied. The irrigation has to be kept going until the air temperature has risen to the point of melting all the ice encasing the buds. I designed tripod stands to support four-metre riser pipes to be able to irrigate over the tops of the trees. We installed enough pipework to cover all the fruit trees in the most susceptible lower part of the orchard. An electric alarm was set up in my bedroom on the farm, connected to an outside thermometer, to warn me of an impending frost, giving me time to get up and go down to the pump house to get the overhead frost irrigation going once the temperature had fallen adequately below freezing point. The irrigation would then be run until the frost had cleared and the dawn temperature risen to allow me to turn off the pump. The one downside of this frost-prevention approach was that we were applying a lot of water to trees that did not need it at that time of the year!

*The morning following a night's frost irrigation with icicles hanging on the branches. An irrigation tripod standpipe can be seen three rows further into the orchard. Water was still being applied until most of the ice had dissolved as the temperature rose.*

During these early years all the fruit harvested at Frilford had to be taken back to the main farm at Kingston Bagpuize to be cold-stored before grading and dispatch to markets at Brentford in London and up north to Leeds or Newcastle upon Tyne.

In 1969 Marshall Bowey, the small dairy farmer who had bought the reduced-sized farm from my father in 1959, had likewise become aware of the land's limitations to provide him with enough good summer hay and adequate all-year-round grazing; so he decided to sell the farm and move down to Dorset, where he could buy a bigger farm on a more water-retentive soil that would provide plenty of summer hay and grass all the year round for a larger dairy herd.

*Mary Clarke (standing) and Janet Grey with her young son Brian enjoying a well-earned break from apple picking, circa 1968. They are seated in front of the large plywood bulk Simven pallet bin, which held 600 pounds of fruit when full. In the background is the Ford 3000 tractor with its simple forklift waiting to load the bins at the end of the afternoon.*

*Three full bins of apples awaiting transport to cold storage. The low-level trailer was a professional conversion from a Second World War bomb trolley.*

By 1969 I had expanded the acreage of land that I was renting locally to grow sweetcorn to over thirty acres. Unfortunately, some of this rented land was not in the best of condition and thus some of these crops did not produce good yields. The chance to buy back the land that my father had sold ten years previously was an opportunity not to be missed. Another local farmer, who had also expressed an interest in purchasing the land, very kindly stood aside when he heard of my interest. I was able, with help from my father and an agricultural mortgage, to secure the purchase, thus reuniting the farm back to its 1959 size.

In the intervening years this farm had become somewhat neglected; upon repurchase we had a lot of tidying-up to do – the disposal of a lot of derelict machinery, rotting piles of old bales and the numerous old wooden pigsties, which had not been used for a very long time, all had to be dismantled and burnt along with an amazing amount of general debris that had accumulated during the ten years since we had last seen the farm.

However, the farmer had erected a new Crendon concrete-framed and asbestos-roofed open-sided cattle barn, which we soon enclosed with windows, walls and doors to convert it into a well-lit pack house; it continues to this day to be used for the same purpose. This style of farm building was very popular at that time and it remains a very sound, strong building.

The worst neglect was the condition of the land. Most of the land had been put down to pasture, which had become heavily infested with couch grass. It took a lot of time and gallons of spray chemicals to clear all the fields of couch before I could consider planting crops of sweetcorn. However, by the following spring enough land had been cleared of the couch to enable me to plant twenty-eight acres of sweetcorn, correspondingly reducing most of the acreage of land that I had been renting locally. By the following year (1971) I was able to plant most of the sweetcorn on my own land.

At the time of writing, we have now grown sweetcorn for fifty-four consecutive years.

*A view down the lane into the farmyard at the time of our repurchase of the farm in the autumn of 1969. Note the piles of manure outside the stable, the loose hay in the open barn and rotting bales piled outside the new Crendon concrete cattle barn. Rank weed growth everywhere hid quantities of rubbish that had to be cleared away in the following months. All the loose hay in the barn had to be baled before we could sell it to clear out the barn to become a temporary machinery store.*

*The same view down the lane twenty years later, in 1989.*

*The author picking sweetcorn into a haversack container which he had designed to speed and ease the work. Once the haversack is full the wearer walks out of the crop and empties the bag, by undoing a drawstring at the bottom of the bag. The haversack contains about sixty cobs. The author has kept quiet about his design, so it remains a unique way of hand-harvesting sweetcorn.*

During this same period I still had adequate confidence in the future of fruit growing to extend the acreage of orchards with the planting of a further eight acres of new apple varieties, so long as I avoided growing the apple variety Golden Delicious, which was then flooding in from very productive orchards in France. There were already signs that the British Government wanted to reduce the existing trade barriers that prevented our markets from being oversupplied with cheap fruit and vegetable supplies from the continent, particularly from France, Italy and Spain.

Throughout the early 1970s there was an excellent government grant scheme, administered by the Ministry of Agriculture, to encourage farmers to modernise their buildings, machinery and production to be ready to compete with our continental neighbours once we joined the EU. I took advantage of this scheme to buy better equipment; but especially to help fund the conversion of the interior of one of the existing nineteenth-century stone barns into a modern cold store for our apple and pear crops.

*The first fruit cold store built into the existing corn barn in 1970, with its pair of large insulated wooden doors. Internally, Thermalite block walls were constructed with a foam-filled cavity to provide a very good level of insulation. To the right is the old stable converted into a cottage.*

As the 1970s progressed, a range of other horticultural crops were introduced onto the farm and expanded according to their profitability. With the introduction of potato growing, more winter cold-storage space was needed. I was again able to obtain generous grant aid to build a new cold store on a site adjacent to the best stone barn on the farm, which had been built about 100 years earlier. This new building was constructed from Thermalite insulation blocks, rendered on the outside, and with an attractive traditional pitched roof tiled with Lincolnshire pantiles, bought from a disused-tile yard beside the River Humber. I felt it was very important that the new building should blend in with the red tiles on the adjacent nineteenth-century stone barn.

*The second fruit and potato cold store built in 1983. A grant-aided new building with rendered, double-thickness, Thermalite block walls under a Lincolnshire pantile roof, to blend in with the neighbouring barn. A washroom/toilet is at the left end and the refrigeration equipment is in the room on the right. Between are three open bays for the storage of machinery.*

It was the start of a long run of annual potato crops, which were to make a staggering impact during the two notorious drought years of 1975 and 1976. By then we had the ability to irrigate all crops according to their needs. In those two drought years we applied all the water necessary to achieve superb yields of excellent-quality potatoes; they sold for very high prices, which we have not witnessed since!

The two very profitable potato years enabled the purchase of a lot of extra new machinery and the upgrading of other aspects of the farm, which have had an enduring benefit to the farm – especially in view of some of the low-profit years that were to follow.

During the mid 1980s we divided two of the largest fields into four smaller ones by planting thick hawthorn hedges. This gave a lot more protection for the crops, providing a better microclimate, free from direct wind damage. Other hawthorn hedges were planted on other parts of the farm for the same reason. Over half a mile of hedges and a similar length of poplar windbreaks, plus a belt of woodland trees, were planted to transform the landscape in this small part of the parish. Over the road the Carter family, who were developing the 'pick-your-own' fruit and vegetable site, carried out similar windbreak planting.

*Potato harvesting beside the A415 in 1985, before the purchase of a complete harvester. The crop was lifted by a two-row elevator digger, which left the potatoes lying cleanly on the surface ready to be hand-picked by the gang of women with their plastic baskets into the bulk bins. The variety being harvested was Estima, a high-yielding second early variety that stored well into winter.*

In 1983 we installed the first stretch of five-inch underground irrigation pipe to take the water up from the pump house beside the stream to the higher ground to reduce heavy water-pressure losses from use of smaller-bore portable pipes. By 1988 the need to irrigate in a number of different fields at any one time was putting a pressure on the time taken to move numerous portable aluminium irrigation pipes around the farm, so the decision was taken to install a four-inch underground main feeder pipe around the farm that would have standpipes in the corner of each main field. We bought all the requisite heavy-duty plastic pipes and fittings, hired a mobile trenching machine and set to work to install this long underground pipe from the stream-side pump house to six selected positions that would provide access to all the fields. This work greatly speeded up the ability to water different crops in different fields on the same day.

For most of the time we have been irrigating crops we have used robust sprinklers, mounted on top of half-metre risers, fixed into the three-inch aluminium water pipes laid out in the crop. In 1997 we purchased an Italian-built Pett mobile irrigator to add to the sprinkler irrigation equipment. The mobile irrigator gave more flexibility and could be moved across a crop quicker than the time taken to move the portable sprinkler lines. The boom irrigator applies water much more evenly than the sprinkler pattern, which is susceptible to wind disturbance and hence uneven water application.

*The Italian-built Pett mobile irrigator. The trolley-mounted twenty-metre boom is attached to a flexible hose that unwinds from the reel as the trolley is pulled out to the end of the field to be irrigated. When the irrigator is set to run, most of the water goes down the pipe to feed the jets along the boom; but a small quantity of water is fed, under pressure, through a turbine that drives the reel-in mechanism to rewind the flexible pipe back onto the reel, so irrigating the crop as the boom trolley is slowly drawn back through the crop.*

Other vegetable crops tried on a reasonable scale included globe artichokes, Dutch white cabbage and summer-sown Japanese bulb onions, together with a wide range of summer salad crops, each of the latter grown on a much smaller scale – crops such as mangetout peas, garlic, Rose Coco beans and different types of cabbage and summer lettuce.

In addition to these shorter-term crops, we have grown a two-acre crop of asparagus for the past twenty-six years. This crop is ideally suited to the light sandy land and during the early years of cropping we were hard put at times to keep up with daily harvesting of spears during its hectic six-week cropping period. In recent years the crop has aged and yields declined sharply, which has been a relief!

Our ability to produce good vegetable crops came to the attention of a local tree nursery (Radclive Nurseries, at Faringdon) which was growing large quantities of trees and shrubs for sale to the development corporations building new towns at Milton Keynes, Cumbernauld and Glenrothes. They needed to expand their production to meet these needs from a home-grown source. We had most of the necessary equipment already to take on this contract production, which began with a small planting in 1973 and slowly expanded to the point where we were lining out an average of twelve to fourteen acres of native hedge and tree species, which amounted to a production of over 600,000 transplants each year.

At one point in the late 1980s we rented an adjacent field for a couple of seasons, which took production up to over a million plants each winter. We were unable to sustain this output due to the amount of time lost during predictable wet periods in the winter, which impeded lifting of the plants; and the nursery, in turn, was having delay problems getting the plants on to the new town sites for the same reasons. We grew, under contract, for this nursery for a total of twenty-five years.

With the end of our plant contract production in sight, in 1998 the nursery kindly allowed me to start selling some of their plants to people who wished to buy direct from me. I kept a careful record and reimbursed them accordingly. This enabled me to begin building up my own client base of customers, so that when the contract finally came to an end I was able to continue production with my own plants and begin selling solely on my own account. I have been growing and selling my own crops of hedge plants ever since.

*A crop of young hawthorn seedlings lined out in four-row beds. By the end of the summer these will have grown into 90–120-cm tall transplants ready for lifting and sale. Chemical weed control keeps the beds clean all season.*

Soon after the original tree nursery withdrew, I was approached by another local tree nursery (Nicholson Nurseries, at North Aston) to do the same style of contract hedge-plant production on a smaller scale. I was very happy to take on this new contract as my own production was still at a low level; thus having their plants to grow alongside my own gave me the economies of scale that were necessary to make the overall crop profitable and to be able to invest in new specialist machinery as necessary. I grew crops for this nursery for a further fourteen years, until they in turn withdrew, because their market was declining with the reduction of government-funded hedge and woodland planting grants.

*Harvesting a good crop of hawthorn transplants. In the foreground the tractor-mounted lifter has undercut the bed of plants and shaken off all the earth, leaving the plants lying on the surface to be picked up and placed in the wooden cage behind the author and his assistant Colin, who is holding a bundle of well-rooted plants.*

These excellent grants had been introduced to counter the extensive hedge removal that had taken place since the end of the last war. At the end of the Second World War farmers had been given grant incentives to increase agricultural production, which they had achieved with great success. The increase in output was achieved by a number of factors, but increased mechanisation played a major part in this transformation – bigger machines needed bigger fields to work in effectively; so hedges and field boundaries were removed and land drained on a large scale. Later on farmers took to burning unwanted straw in the field, which led to considerable damage to adjacent hedges being scorched or burnt whenever the straw burning was mismanaged or simply got out of control. At a later date a straw-burning ban was imposed, but not before thousands of hedges had suffered.

*Adrian and Colin grading hawthorn plants in the well-lit pack house. The plants are checked and placed onto the conveyor-belt grader, which is marked with lines to denote different plant heights. The plants are then placed on side tables, according to height, to be counted and machine-bundled.*

My own production and sale of hedge and tree transplants has likewise declined slowly in recent years with the reduction of hedgerow renewal and planting grants; but it has come at a time when I wanted to reduce cropping on the farm, as I move towards retirement.

It is worth returning to the theme of land-use changes in the parish as time has progressed. The range of crops and their rotation within the parish had remained remarkably consistent and little changed for nearly 1,000 years! – remaining unchanged right up to the point when my father began planting an orchard in 1960. Up to this point crops had been selected upon their ability to cope with the inherent light, and dry, soil conditions. Beyond the addition of farmyard manure and, latterly, basic organic fertilisers such as guano, lime and superphosphate, the crops had to fend for themselves. Yields would vary from year to year according to the weather conditions, the farmer having limited ability to influence the outcome. Consequently, runs of dry summers would reduce yields, leaving the farmer with little or no profit on many an occasion.

With the planting of an orchard at Frilford, my father had not only introduced a crop that had never been grown in the parish before, but along with it came new ways to influence the health, growth and final yield. We were able to apply a range of spray chemicals to protect the crop from the predation of pests and diseases.

*Spraying young fruit trees with a new Drake & Fletcher Victair sprayer in 1964. The fan-assisted jets are arranged around the air outlet to give a good distribution to the trees on either side.*

We were able to water the crop in dry times to ensure good growth and fruit yields. We could apply herbicides to control weed growth around the trees. All these cultural aids had not been available to previous generations of farmers. Probably the most significant benefit has been the ability to irrigate our crops. The inherent poor moisture retention of the light sandy soil was no longer a limiting factor in obtaining good growth and higher yields. In fact these light soils, which often dried up in summer, could now be watered as required giving us the benefit of early spring crop establishment and growth, plus earlier harvests; this would often result in a better market price, where an early harvest brought a premium over later crops from other producers.

Some years after we had begun to grow irrigated fruit and vegetable crops in Frilford, the farmer on the other side of the main road also went down a similar path. Where he had been growing modest crops of cereals, he now established a thriving farm shop, growing a very wide range of soft fruits and vegetables – all thanks to his ability to irrigate the crops with water drawn from nearby springs or from the River Ock at the bottom of the farm, which ran along the southern parish boundary.

The planting of intensive horticultural crops on both our land and that of the neighbour mentioned above was accompanied by the planting of hedges and rows of windbreak trees to protect the crops from the prevailing south-west wind blowing across this otherwise historic open-field landscape, mentioned earlier. There are still parts of the parish where the open-field nature remains, to show one what the landscape would have looked like historically; today a larger part of the parish is now enclosed with hedges and shelter belts of trees, to provide a better climate for the new fruit and vegetable crops.

I have mentioned the rotation of crops, but have not specifically explained why this is done. The two main reasons for rotating crops are to minimise the build-up of harmful soil-borne pests and diseases and to maintain and improve the soil's health and fertility. The earliest cultivators did not understand this important aspect of crop husbandry. Those who first cleared the land to grow crops found that after several years their grain yields began to diminish. Their response was to move on, clear fresh ground, and start again; so they slowly moved across the landscape as each area of cropping land became disease-ridden and denuded of nutrients. Eventually later generations of early farmers became aware of what was happening and overcame the problem by resting the land for a year or two before returning to crop it again. The land being rested was kept free of weeds by grazing it with their cattle, sheep and pigs. This action fertilised the soil with the dung dropped by the animals and the passage of time would diminish any soil diseases that had built up during the previous cropping.

*A view up the central farm track soon after the repurchase of the farm in 1969. Note the open-field landscape unaltered for centuries.*

Once the early farmers had recognised the basics of crop hygiene by resting or rotating their crops, they no longer had to live a nomadic lifestyle, moving on to freshly cleared virgin ground every few years. They could now choose where to establish permanent communities, which were close to the land they cultivated each year. These settlements would also be sited close to a water source, both for their own needs and for those of their livestock; the latter requiring a greater daily need for drinking water.

*The same view up the central farm track twenty years later in 1989.*
*A mature poplar windbreak avenue has been established.*

These principles remain the bedrock of sustainable agricultural production. We continue to run the risk of denuding our soils by mono-cropping land year after year.

At Frilford, we too realised that by growing the same,

profitable, crops with only short rotations we were running the risk of increased soil diseases. In our case this became an issue as we tried to minimise the rotational break between the two most valuable crops, of potatoes and hedge plants. We knew that the popular hedge species hawthorn, in particular, was very prone to reduced growth vigour when planted more than once every five to ten years on the same site. At the same time the potato crop would also infect the land with its own range of soil-borne diseases, which were also particularly dangerous to the hedge plant crop. We thus had two potentially profitable crops that both needed long rotational breaks. We had enough land to do this, but needed to introduce a further 'new' crop to rest the land before, or after, each of these two important main crops. In 1976, after the second superb potato year, we introduced winter wheat to the rotation. In addition to resting the land, the wheat crop gave us a good opportunity to control any problem weeds partly by applying the requisite herbicide spray and by the ability of the densely sown crop to smother out a lot of weed competition.

In 1981 we experimented with growing thatching straw. We purchased a small vintage Massey-Harris binder from a retired farmer in Standlake and fully restored it to good working order, but were unable to grow the crop tall enough on our light land; so the idea was abandoned after one season.

We grew varying wheat crops for twenty years until the poor market price combined with increasing problems with handling and storing such a crop on a small scale made it unviable to continue.

Towards the end of the time growing mostly winter wheat, we grew a few crops of spring wheat, hoping to be able to produce a more valuable sample that could be sold for milling, rather than the usual destination of our winter wheat onto the animal-feed market. A local miller approached us for small supplies of milling-quality wheat. He had restored the nearby historic undershot mill on the little River Ock, beside the A338, a couple of miles down the road, in the next parish, and needed small quantities for stone-grinding demonstrations on his open

*The restored five-foot-cut binder drawn behind a tractor. The binder was driven by a large steel drive wheel on the far side of the elevator.*

*Paul Paintin stooks the sheaves into groups of eight to dry.*

days and to be able to sell the surplus of this flour to local shops. For a couple of years we were able to offer him supplies, until we stopped growing wheat altogether.

*Paul Weaving's combine cutting a spring-wheat crop of the variety Spark. We were very fortunate to have Paul's services to cut every crop of wheat that we grew over a period of twenty-eight years. He would put aside cutting his own crops to come and cut our crop on a day when it was dry enough to be stored without the need for any further drying.*

As I move towards retirement, cropping on Collins Farm has been reduced to smaller acreages of hedge plants, sweetcorn, asparagus and Christmas trees. The remainder of the land has been put down to grass. One grass field is let to a club that fly model helicopters, another to a grower of strawberry plants. The remainder are sown to grass and once again being grazed by sheep brought in by a local farming couple. This will ensure the fertility and cleanliness of the land for whatever future use comes along.

*A Ford four-wheel drive tractor pulling a three-furrow plough with slatted mould boards and a trailed furrow press. It is ploughing in mown stubble following a wheat crop. This small tractor is able to pull all this equipment partly because of the easy-working light soil and because the slats on the mould boards reduce friction as well as breaking up the soil as it passes over the slats. The trailed furrow press compresses the ploughed land flat to ease subsequent cultivations.*

# 6

# THE FUTURE FOR FRILFORD AND COLLINS FARM

I have mentioned that my time as an active farmer is drawing to a close, but that will have been little more than a blink of an eye in the history of this farm and the surrounding parish.

The landscape of Frilford and the fortunes of this farm will continue to change and unfold. The United Kingdom has recently voted to leave the European Union with consequences that are largely unknown. It is safe to say that the farming community will have to adjust to harsher times ahead. As members of the EEC, British farmers have fared quite well as our French farming neighbours have vigorously defended their rural existence, obtaining a larger slice of the community budget for agriculture across Europe than might be good for the community as a whole.

The UK Government no longer regards agriculture as a keystone to national food security, preferring to allow increasing food imports to flow in to keep food prices as low as possible. This policy is further enhanced by the rise of the supermarkets, who now dominate the bulk of food distribution across the country and hence are able to hold producers to ransom in their drive to reduce food prices as they compete with each other for a share of a largely static market.

When I began farming there were numerous small greengrocers in towns and villages with local wholesalers supplying these shops daily with all their needs for fresh produce. Most of these greengrocers have now disappeared and with them has gone the network of small wholesalers that supplied them. To move the volume of sweetcorn that I continue to grow, I have to deliver to larger remaining wholesalers further afield. Most of the produce that I now take to the Evesham area ends up being sold into the West Country; the wholesaler runs large articulated delivery lorries down into Devon and Cornwall each night.

The neighbouring farm shop continues to sell a wide range of fruit and vegetables to visiting customers, but even they have to find markets further afield to sell the balance of their production, because all the local supermarkets are locked into selling produce that is delivered to them from their central warehouses, which are in turn supplied by large contracted growers across the country.

There are ever reducing opportunities for small local growers to supply to local markets – the advent of farmers' markets provides only a limited outlet for small quantities of produce. Any grower wishing to grow larger quantities of produce will have to compete for the demanding bulk requirements of the supermarket trade.

The land will continue to grow crops to feed the nation, but the pattern of production and distribution will continue to adapt to meet fast-changing times.

It is the speed of change that makes it hard to predict what the future holds for both Collins Farm and the landscape of Frilford; but both will have a future.

# 7

## TAILPIECE

I could not leave out of the book this lovely photo taken by Eric Guy, a well-known commercial photographer who worked across the southern counties from the 1930s to the 1960s capturing rural life for magazines such as *Farmers' Weekly*.

It is titled 'Taking care of the implements – a new elevator seen in a field at Frilford, near Abingdon – 5th Oct. 1951.'

The photograph, taken beside the main road (A415), shows the open landscape across Collins Farm, with the enclosure hawthorn hedge across the field, and numerous elm trees in the distance.

*Photo of a wooden elevator, protected with a thatched straw cover in a field at Collins Farm in 1951. The photo was taken from the roadside by the respected commercial photographer Eric Guy.*

# BIBLIOGRAPHY

Gelling, M., and Cole, A. – *The Landscape of Place-Names* – Shaun Tyas, Stamford, 2000.

Hall, David – *Medieval Fields* – Shire Publications Ltd, Princes Risborough, Bucks, HP17 9AJ, 1982.

Hoskins, W. G. – *The Making of the English Landscape* – Book Club Associates, London, 1981.

Lisle, E. – *Observations in Husbandry* – Faulkner, Essex Street, Dublin, 1757.

Markham, G. – *Farewell to Husbandry* – Paternoster Row, London, 1638.

Mavor, William – *A General View of the Agriculture of Berkshire* – The Board of Agriculture, printed for Richard Phillips, London, 1809.

Orwin, C. S. – *The Open Fields* (3rd edition) – Oxford University Press, London Wl, 1967.

Rothamsted Experimental Station – *Soils of the Wantage & Abingdon District* – Richard Clay (The Chaucer Press) Ltd, Bungay, Suffolk, 1973.

Worlidge, John – *Systema Agriculturae – The Mystery of Husbandry Discovered* – Fleet Street, London, 1681.

# ACKNOWLEDGEMENTS

My thanks go to:

Berkshire Records Office, Coley Avenue, Reading, Berkshire, for information on the enclosure movement, with particular reference to Frilford, including the use of its enclosure maps.

Historic England, for permission to use the wartime (1944) aerial survey photo.

Chris Honeywell, for preparing all the illustrations for the publisher, and for taking some of the photos required.

The Museum of English Rural Life, Reading, Berkshire, for permission to use a photo by Eric Guy.

Valerie Petts for kindly drawing three maps.

Elisabeth Whitehouse, from Marcham, for her help with local historical information, gleaned from her detailed and substantial researches into local people and places.

William Wintle, for providing a lot of data and printed information regarding his researches into Roman Britain in the Vale of the White Horse, with special reference to the Frilford area. He also kindly provided the geophysical images.

My wife, for corrections and suggestions to the text.